STEP INTO THE FAST LANE

Since 1968, Hot Wheels® has produced over five billion cars. If you put them all back to back, that's enough cars to circle the world four times! From scale versions of classic hot rods and speedy drag racers to wild, souped-up fantasy cars, there are vehicles to inspire collectors and kids alike.

Among those billions of cars, there are some that have themes that make them fun to collect, such as the mini collection cars. There are others that are rarer or more special—Treasure Hunt or Super Treasure Hunt cars. Discover what makes these cars some of the most exclusive in the Hot Wheels® lineup and how to identify them by their packaging and paint schemes.

Get facts and stats on over 150 Hot Wheels® cars and learn about Hot Wheels® history, signature parts, and what it takes to become a Hot Wheels® collector. It's time to hit the accelerator and drive into the extraordinary world of Hot Wheels®!

TABLE OF CONTENTS

DID YOU KNOW?

AS FAST AS A MISSILE!

Hot Wheels® vehicles can clock some fast times going down those plastic ramps. It's no wonder they are built for speed—Jack Ryan, one of the original Hot Wheels® engineers, previously designed missiles at Raytheon!

A TIMELESS CLASSIC

The Custom Camaro, in a dark blue, was one of the first Hot Wheels® cars ever produced and has remained one of the most popular. It was recast for Hot Wheels® 25th anniversary in 1993 and continues to appear as part of the regular line.

A WHOLE WORLD OF COLLECTORS!

Hotwheelscollectors.com is the largest die-cast collector community on the Internet with more than 275,000 users.

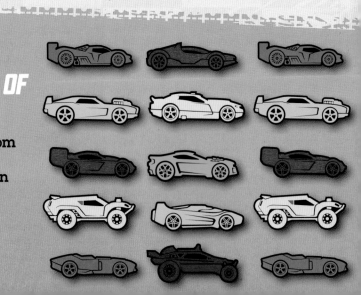

A TOWN CALLED SPEED!

On August 6, 2006, more than 10,000 die-cast car enthusiasts converged on the 0.2-square-mile town of Speed, Kansas, for the ultimate Hot Wheels® festival.

SPEED →

DIAMONDS ARE FOREVER!

To celebrate Hot Wheels® 40th anniversary and the production of the four billionth Hot Wheels® car, celebrity jeweler Jason of Beverly Hills created a one-of-a-kind, 1:64-scale jewel-studded Hot Wheels® car valued at $140,000, which was auctioned off for charity.

HOW HOT WHEELS® GOT ITS NAME

When Elliott Handler, cofounder of Mattel, saw ace designer Harry Bradley's classic Southern California hot rod in the parking lot, he said, "Man, those are some Hot Wheels!" and thus, the world-famous toy car company was born.

HOT WHEELS® HISTORY: SIGNATURE STYLE

Hot Wheels® cars feature a variety of unique features that set them apart from other cars. These features started with the original sixteen cars produced by Hot Wheels®. These features are now found on a selection of special collectible cars.

REDLINE WHEELS

In the beginning, Hot Wheels® cars were manufactured with a red strip on the tires—these cars were referred to as "Redlines." Hot Wheels® stopped including the red stripe on the wheels in 1978, but red striped wheels returned in 1993 on certain vintage reproductions of the originals.

SPECTRAFLAME™ PAINT

When Hot Wheels® first started, they used a special paint called Spectraflame to give their cars a metallic shine. Wild Spectraflame™ colors, such as Candy Apple, Antifreeze Green, Ice Blue, and Hot Pink, were an instant hit with collectors!

BEARINGS

Jack Ryan, the original head of research and development for Hot Wheels®, is responsible for creating remarkably good bearings for Hot Wheels® cars. An expert in high-tech materials, he was able to make bearings for Hot Wheels® cars, one of the most important features in terms of speed and performance. As they say, "Horsepower sells the car, but bearings win the race!"

MAG WHEELS

In order for Hot Wheels® cars to go as fast as possible, Hot Wheels® began by making their wheels out of a low-friction durable plastic called Delrin. These low-friction wheels make it possible for Hot Wheels® cars to go up to scale 200 mph!

WORKING SUSPENSION

Mattel engineer Howard Newman designed the original suspension systems based on real-life race cars, which gave Hot Wheels® cars shock absorbency and wheel bounce. In 1970, the suspension system was improved upon with solid axles mounted on a plastic bar, which acted as a spring.

DESIGNER PARTS

SPOILERS

Rear spoilers allow better airflow over and around the car, which gives a car better traction and handling when racing.

TAILFINS

Inspired by the look of World War II fighter planes, tailfins add a bit of flair to any car.

EXHAUST PIPES

Whether exhaust pipes come out the back, out the sides, or wrap around to the top, they not only vent fumes from the engine, but create a bold statement.

From fins and fangs to fancy grilles, Hot Wheels® cars have featured some eye-popping car parts to give them their unique looks!

TINTED WINDOWS

Not only do tinted windows create privacy, they can be tinted a variety of colors to give your car extra sass.

COWL INDUCTION HOOD

This type of hood has an opening to force air into the engine to keep it cool—it also creates added style!

GRILLE

Often resembling teeth or a mouth, the front grille lets air enter while still protecting the engine.

COLLECT THEM ALL

Each year there are new collections and car designs. For collectors, it's important to know what kind of cars you have. The fastest way to find out is right on the package!

SERIES NUMBER

This is the collector number for the year the car was released.

BEST FOR TRACK

This means the car works especially well in track sets.

MINI COLLECTION NUMBER

This indicates the number of cars in the mini collection.

MINI COLLECTION ICON

This is an easy way to tell which mini collection the car belongs to.

MINI COLLECTION NAME

This is the official name of the mini collection.

VEHICLE NAME

This is the official name of the vehicle.

TREASURE HUNT
QUICK GUIDE

Look for these icons on the pages to find out what year a car was a Treasure Hunt car and which ones were Super Treasure Hunt vehicles.

Treasure Hunt cars have a special flame logo in the paint designs, which make them rare.

Super Treasure Hunts are upgraded versions of basic cars. They have Spectraflame paint and a special TH logo in the paint design. Keep an eye out for this TH symbol in the following pages. It marks which cars are Super Treasure Hunts.

TH

MINI COLLECTION
QUICK GUIDE

Look for these icons on the following pages to find out which mini collection a car belongs to.

  **HW Ride-Ons™** are designed so that you can attach mini figures.

 **Then and Now®** are pairs of cars—the classic model and the modern update.

 **HW Snow Stormers™** are chilled out and ready to take on the powder.

HW Green Speed™ are solar-powered and electric cars that prove you don't need gas to speed past the competition.

  **HW Rescue™** are fast, fearless, and ready to save the day.

Sky Show® are show planes and copters, plus their transport vehicles.

Super Chromes® are mirrorlike cars that shine on the track.

HW Moto™ are dream bikes and two-wheeled favorites.

HW Daredevils™ are stunt vehicles that push the limits of speed with souped-up design.

X-Raycers® are not only fast on the tracks, they have see-through bodies and wheels.

HW Flames™ are voted for by fans online, and all of them feature cool flame details.

HW Hot Trucks® are 4x4s and trucks that are ready to work or race.

HW Speed Graphics™ are real race performers that hit high speeds on the track.

DRIVERS, REV YOUR ENGINES!

MINI COLLECTIONS

Whether it is an eco-friendly Green Racer, a hardworking Hot Truck, a trail-blazing Snow Stormer™, or a cutting-edge X-Raycer®, these themed vehicles have what it takes to get the job done!

CUSTOM '72 CHEVROLET® LUV™
HW HOT TRUCKS™

TREASURE HUNT & SUPER TREASURE HUNT CARS

Hard to find and even harder to beat! Hot Wheels® Treasure Hunt and Super Treasure Hunt cars are more than worth the search! Keep your eyes out for these secret collector's items.

STING ROD II®
2013 TREASURE HUNT

MINI COLLECTIONS

Join the Club!

What happens when Hot Wheels® designers let their imaginations run wild? Turn the page to see cool cars, including amphibious hybrid vehicles, stealthy spy cars, cars that fly, and monster work trucks, to name just a few. Whatever it takes to get the job done and have fun, there's a Hot Wheels® car ready to take it on!

CLOAK AND DAGGER®
X-RAYCER®

19

MINI COLLECTIONS

VANDETTA®

BIRTHPLACE: El Segundo, CA
DESIGNER: Hot Wheels®
SPECIALTY: Those oversized rear wheels help it handle an extra serving of horsepower. This tuner-style speeder inspired by European racers is out for vengeance.

PHARADOX™

BIRTHPLACE: El Segundo, CA

DESIGNER: Hot Wheels®

SPECIALTY: With a triangular grill and sleek hood, this ancient Egyptian-style car is customized with a hidden hieroglyphic of the Hot Wheels® logo.

FAST FACT

The cockpit of the Pharadox™ is shaped like an ancient Egyptian beard!

STOCKAR

BIRTHPLACE: El Segundo, CA

DESIGNER: Hot Wheels®

SPECIALTY: Set the track on fire with Stockar! It's "clear" to see where this racer gets its power. Check out that V8 engine.

RACE OVER TO PAGE 75 TO SEE THE TREASURE HUNT VERSION.

21

CLEAR SPEEDER®

BIRTHPLACE: El Segundo, CA
DESIGNER: Hot Wheels®
SPECIALTY: Here's a sleek, executive-level speeder with an eye to the future. Top and bottom are fully transparent—no surprises here—and it's ready to lead the pack.

BLITZSPEEDER™

BIRTHPLACE: El Segundo, CA
DESIGNER: Hot Wheels®
SPECIALTY: Time to head to the track! With its rear wing stabilizer and front-mounted V8, 700 HP engine, the Blitzspeeder™ will take you straight to the leader board!

RIG STORM®

BIRTHPLACE: El Segundo, CA
DESIGNER: Hot Wheels®
SPECIALTY: Harness the power of a tornado with this V12 diesel-powered race truck with loads of torque.

SPEED SLAYER®

BIRTHPLACE: El Segundo, CA

DESIGNER: Hot Wheels®

SPECIALTY: This land-speed champ has two extra-large jet engines and massive air intakes to feed the beast. It's a flat-out leader—ready to destroy the competition.

CLOAK AND DAGGER®

BIRTHPLACE: El Segundo, CA

DESIGNER: Hot Wheels®

SPECIALTY: Made for interplanetary stealth missions, this futuristic single-seater has no windows, covered wheels, and a mini jet engine to make it fly.

FAST FACT

The Cloak and Dagger® car features a removable canopy. The body can be removed to reveal the inner workings of the car.

CHECK OUT THE TREASURE HUNT VERSION ON PAGE 67.

BULLET PROOF®

BIRTHPLACE: El Segundo, CA
DESIGNER: Hot Wheels®
SPECIALTY: Step into action with this double agent speedster! Its techno-armor plating and low profile are super-stealthy.

AERO POD®

BIRTHPLACE: El Segundo, CA
DESIGNER: Hot Wheels®
SPECIALTY: The aerodynamic body allows it to move fast, even in high winds, and the V16 quad turbocharged engine gives it an abundance of torque. Its oversized cargo area lets this ultra hauler carry anything it desires.

'52 HUDSON HORNET

BIRTHPLACE: Auburn Hills, MI
DESIGNER: Chrysler Group, LLC
SPECIALTY: Based on the 1950s NASCAR race car, this Spectraflame red car has tinted windows, a black interior, gold chrome Real Riders® Steelie wheels, and sides covered in yellow and black flames.

'66 FORD 427 FAIRLANE

BIRTHPLACE: Dearborn, MI
DESIGNER: Ford Motor Company
SPECIALTY: With a 427 V8 engine, fiberglass hood with scoop, and two 4-barrel carburetors, this rare racing dragster was made to fly down the fast lane.

FAST FACT

The Ford Fairlane was named after Henry Ford's estate, "Fairlane," just outside of Dearborn, MI.

'69 DODGE CORONET SUPER BEE

BIRTHPLACE: Auburn Hills, MI
DESIGNER: Chrysler Group, LLC
SPECIALTY: Equipped with a powerful engine, optional HEMI®, and heavy-duty suspension, this speed machine will buzz by so fast you might miss the bee logo on the back!

FAST FACT

Car designer Harvey J. Winn won a contest to name the new Dodge model—he entered the name "Super Bee."

'70 CAMARO® ROAD RACE

BIRTHPLACE: Detroit, MI
DESIGNER: General Motors
SPECIALTY: A best in show example of a second generation Camaro, this pony is slick, fast, and ready to show or race!

'77 PONTIAC FIREBIRD T/A

BIRTHPLACE: Detroit, MI
DESIGNER: General Motors
SPECIALTY: With a super-duty 455 V8 engine and its signature egg-crate grille, this high-performance bird knows how to fly!

'67 CHEVELLE

BIRTHPLACE: Detroit, MI
DESIGNER: General Motors
SPECIALTY: With a dual exhaust, hood bulges to show off its power, and a V8 engine, this American muscle classic was made for late night street fights.

'69 MERCURY CYCLONE

BIRTHPLACE: Dearborn, MI
DESIGNER: Ford Motor Company
SPECIALTY: For 1969, Mercury dropped "Comet" from the name, but this classic muscle car is still a whirl-wind racer that represents style and true performance.

'69 DODGE CHARGER

BIRTHPLACE: Auburn Hills, MI
DESIGNER: Chrysler Group, LLC
SPECIALTY: Dramatic styling, heavy-duty suspension, and the 440 CID Magnum make this high-performance classic a winged warrior, built to win.

FAST FACT

If you place a quarter behind the driver's seat of Grass Chomper™, you can pop a wheelie! You can also attach your Mega Bloks® figure!

GRASS CHOMPER™

BIRTHPLACE: El Segundo, CA
DESIGNER: Hot Wheels®
SPECIALTY: Get chomping! With powerful twin blades and a supercharged engine, the Grass Chomper™ will mow your lawn in no time!

PEDAL DRIVER®

BIRTHPLACE: El Segundo, CA
DESIGNER: Hot Wheels®
SPECIALTY: With a blown engine and side exhaust, this single-seat pedal racer is geared up to pound the competition.

LET'S GO™

BIRTHPLACE: El Segundo, CA
DESIGNER: Hot Wheels®
SPECIALTY: Strap in your mini-fig for the ride of its life! "Let's GO" a kartin'!

FIG RIG®

BIRTHPLACE: El Segundo, CA
DESIGNER: Hot Wheels®
SPECIALTY: Exposed air intakes make this speedy street pickup rigged for power! Plus riders are welcome with fig passenger notches and spots to hang on.

'68 SHELBY GT500™

BIRTHPLACE: Ionia, MI
DESIGNER: Shelby American and Ford Motor Company
SPECIALTY: With a 428 ci V8 engine rated at 360 hp, a built-in roll cage, and an aggressive front end, this Shelby is fast, agile, and ready to tear up the drag strip.

FAST FACT

In April 1968, Ford began factory installing a version of the 428 engine known as the "Cobra Jet." The GT500 was known from then on as the GT500-KR.

CUSTOM '15 FORD MUSTANG

BIRTHPLACE: Dearborn, MI
DESIGNER: Ford Motor Company
SPECIALTY: It has a large rear wing to help gain downforce on the corners and a souped-up, supercharged V8 under the hood. Custom-tuned classic pony is ready to race!

'71 DODGE CHALLENGER

THEN NOW

BIRTHPLACE: Auburn Hills, MI

DESIGNER: Chrysler Group, LLC

SPECIALTY: Dodge scored a pony car hit with this warrior! It's a force to be reckoned with on all fronts—be it street, strip, or track.

FAST FACT

A pony car is a compact sports car inspired by the Ford Mustang—which is how this type of car got the name "pony."

'15 DODGE CHALLENGER SRT

THEN NOW

BIRTHPLACE: Auburn Hills, MI

DESIGNER: Chrysler Group, LLC

SPECIALTY: This updated-yet-retro version of an old favorite, with an 8-speed automatic transmission and a massive motor, is strong, fast, and better than ever.

CORVETTE® GRAND SPORT™ ROADSTER

BIRTHPLACE: Detroit, MI, USA

DESIGNER: General Motors

SPECIALTY: One of only five like it, this hand-built version has thin layers of fiberglass on the body and aluminum underneath, making it superlight. This roadster was made to race, and to win.

'14 CORVETTE® STINGRAY™

BIRTHPLACE: Detroit, MI

DESIGNER: General Motors

SPECIALTY: With nearly 450 hp, this styling racer is sure to leave its competition with a sting!

RACE TO PAGE 89 TO SEE THE TREASURE HUNT VERSION.

CLOUD CUTTER™

BIRTHPLACE: El Segundo, CA
DESIGNER: Hot Wheels®
SPECIALTY: Looking like a fighter jet on wheels, with a single-seat cockpit, this aerodynamic racer is ready to soar.

MAD PROPZ®

BIRTHPLACE: El Segundo, CA
DESIGNER: Hot Wheels®
SPECIALTY: Designed after the Curtiss P-40 Warhawk Fighter, this high-flying stunt plane is mad fun!

SKYFIRE®

BIRTHPLACE: El Segundo, CA
DESIGNER: Hot Wheels®
SPECIALTY: With its dual cockpit window and racing number, this helicopter is ready to set the skies on fire!

HW FORMULA SOLAR™

BIRTHPLACE: El Segundo, CA

DESIGNER: Hot Wheels®

SPECIALTY: This aerodynamic, solar-powered speeder is made to race. Its dual electronic motors are solar powered. The open body exposes the charging system and cockpit. It's electric!

SUPER VOLT

BIRTHPLACE: Detroit, MI

DESIGNER: General Motors

SPECIALTY: This souped-up Chevrolet Volt is an electric favorite. Check out the blown motor and aerodynamic rear spoiler. It's fast, efficient, and loaded with style.

POWER SURGE™

BIRTHPLACE: El Segundo, CA

DESIGNER: Hot Wheels®

SPECIALTY: With wireless induction charging coils and oversized heat sinks to power gigantic electric motors, this completely electric supercar is fully charged and ready for anything.

'15 FORD F-150

BIRTHPLACE: Dearborn, MI

DESIGNER: Ford Motor Company

SPECIALTY: This perennial favorite features a powerful 5.0L V8 engine, flex-fuel capabilities, and a lightweight aluminum body, making it the most powerful and efficient F-150 model ever.

FAST FACT

The real Ford F-150 has been the best-selling pickup since 1977. It is also the best-selling vehicle in Canada.

BAD MUDDER™ 2

BIRTHPLACE: El Segundo, CA
DESIGNER: Hot Wheels®
SPECIALTY: With a hood intake scoop, dual stacks, and oversize fenders, this rock crusher was made to take all-terrain to the next level!

TURBINE TIME®

BIRTHPLACE: El Segundo, CA
DESIGNER: Hot Wheels®
SPECIALTY: Featuring dual jet engines out back, this Larry Wood–designed, low-ridin' truck is one crazy-fast beast!

'17 FORD F-150 RAPTOR

BIRTHPLACE: Dearborn, MI
DESIGNER: Ford Motor Company
SPECIALTY: With its performance-tuned suspension system, advanced off-road technology, and increased horsepower, the 2017 Ford F-150 Raptor is ready for any off-road adventure.

'67 CHEVY C10

BIRTHPLACE: Detroit, MI
DESIGNER: General Motors
SPECIALTY: Designed for gettin' the job done, this "Action-Line" Chevy pickup is a true classic.

FAST FACT

Off-Duty® was inspired by Mega-Duty®. Hot Wheels® designers use similar names to pay respect to the cars that inspire them.

OFF-DUTY®

BIRTHPLACE: El Segundo, CA
DESIGNER: Hot Wheels®
SPECIALTY: An all-terrain, lifted pickup with supersized off-road tires, front grille guard, and fog lights—this truck is unstoppable crossing the jungle, desert, or snow!

DODGE RAM 1500

BIRTHPLACE: Auburn Hills, MI
DESIGNER: Chrysler Group, LLC
SPECIALTY: Open up the bed and let the sound system bump! This truck's fat tires, thick tread, and a lift kit make it perfect for off-roading or rambling over river rocks.

DAWGZILLA™

BIRTHPLACE: El Segundo, CA
DESIGNER: Hot Wheels®
SPECIALTY: Loaded with a big-block V8, oversized off-road wheels, and a full-time 4x4 system, this beastly muscle truck always gets the job done.

'72 CHEVY® LUV™

BIRTHPLACE: Detroit, MI
DESIGNER: General Motors
SPECIALTY: This souped-up, decked-out version of a LUV—light utility vehicle—features a sunroof, exposed engine, and plenty of power.

HOT WHEELS HIGH®

BIRTHPLACE: El Segundo, CA
DESIGNER: Hot Wheels®
SPECIALTY: Here's a twin turbine, jet-powered bus that's never late for class. Check out the oversized side and roof windows, designed for watching the world whiz by.

TEEGRAY®

BIRTHPLACE: El Segundo, CA
DESIGNER: Hot Wheels®
SPECIALTY: With twin roof-mounted ear-shaped scoops and air intakes in the side stripes, this mid-engine exotic goes feline fast!

REV ROD®

BIRTHPLACE: El Segundo, CA
DESIGNER: Hot Wheels®
SPECIALTY: Fueled by liquid imagination, this futuristic super car has unparalleled power.

HW POPPA WHEELIE™

BIRTHPLACE: El Segundo, CA
DESIGNER: Hot Wheels®
SPECIALTY: Tricked out with a specially weighted bar and a supercharged V8 engine, this three-wheeled stunt ride is always poppin'.

MONTERACER®

BIRTHPLACE: El Segundo, CA
DESIGNER: Hot Wheels®
SPECIALTY: No roof, no windshield, no problem! This small, lightweight roadster is built for handling the sharp corners and fast straightaways at the track.

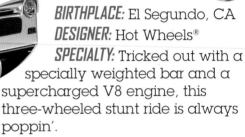

X-STEAM™

BIRTHPLACE: El Segundo, CA
DESIGNER: Hot Wheels®
SPECIALTY: Inside its massive 12-cylinder front burner, water boils to a super-hot 500°, propelling this ultra-unique racer to scorching speeds!

NITRO TAILGATER®

BIRTHPLACE: El Segundo, CA
DESIGNER: Hot Wheels®
SPECIALTY: With six bucket seats, a blown engine, and tons of torque, it's probably the coolest ride in the carpool line.

Z-ROD™

BIRTHPLACE: El Segundo, CA

DESIGNER: Hot Wheels®

SPECIALTY: The direct-injection V6 engine, drivetrain, and body all attach to the z-shaped rails, giving this car more zip than zzzz's.

TWO TIMER®

BIRTHPLACE: El Segundo, CA

DESIGNER: Hot Wheels®

SPECIALTY: Double down on speed with this stylish racer! Check out its dual-plane rear wing for extra downforce and cooling vents over each wheel.

TANKNATOR™!

BIRTHPLACE: El Segundo, CA
DESIGNER: Hot Wheels®
SPECIALTY: Here is a full-blown tank with hot-rod attitude! Rotate the turret and prepare for battle. No one stands a chance against the Tanknator!

TERRAIN STORM™

BIRTHPLACE: El Segundo, CA
DESIGNER: Hot Wheels®
SPECIALTY: Built for the toughest desert rally with an exposed 12-cylinder engine, this buggy is one mean off-roader!

HW450F®

BIRTHPLACE: El Segundo, CA
DESIGNER: Hot Wheels®
SPECIALTY: Unleash your daredevil! With its knobby tires, a custom tailpipe, and longtravel suspension, this trail-blazing bike is perfect for getting down and dirty.

DUNE CRUSHER™

BIRTHPLACE: El Segundo, CA
DESIGNER: Hot Wheels®
SPECIALTY: Made for off-pavement racing, this superfast truck is ready to chew up and spit out any terrain the Baja course serves up.

CRUISE BRUISER™

BIRTHPLACE: El Segundo, CA
DESIGNER: Hot Wheels®
SPECIALTY: This family wagon has been transformed into a hard-knocking, fire-breathing demolition beast. The anchor in the back keeps it from being rocked by the competition!

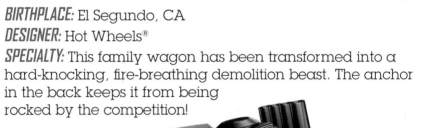

SO PLOWED®

BIRTHPLACE: El Segundo, CA
DESIGNER: Hot Wheels®
SPECIALTY: With an oversized snow blade up front, a V10, and an extra helping of torque, this cold weather beast is built for moving mountains— of snow at least!

ICE SHREDDER®

BIRTHPLACE: El Segundo, CA
DESIGNER: Hot Wheels®
SPECIALTY: Take on the steep, icy slopes at super high speeds in this shark-inspired bobsled!

'12 FORD FIESTA

BIRTHPLACE: Dearborn, MI
DESIGNER: Ford Motor Company
SPECIALTY: This sportier and souped-up version of Ford's popular hatchback is ready to rumble with its front spoiler, chunky side skirts, and a turbocharged four-cylinder engine!

RACE TO PAGE 62 TO SEE THE TREASURE HUNT VERSION.

SNOW STORMER™

BIRTHPLACE: El Segundo, CA
DESIGNER: Hot Wheels®
SPECIALTY: With its extra-wide tracks for super traction and dual exhaust, this winter beast is ready for storming with attitude!

HOVER STORM®

BIRTHPLACE: El Segundo, CA
DESIGNER: Hot Wheels®
SPECIALTY: Designed to race down roads and hover above water, this air-cushioned speeder with twin turbo props and a mid-mounted engine is ready to fly!

'66 FORD TORINO TALLADEGA

BIRTHPLACE: Dearborn, MI

DESIGNER: Ford Motor Company

SPECIALTY: With a V8 engine, a flush-mounted grille, and an extended nose for better aerodynamics, this Ford classic was meant for the track, but made for the street.

FAST FACT

The Ford Torino Talladega was named after Talladega Superspeedway racetrack in Alabama!

DODGE CHALLENGER DRIFT CAR

BIRTHPLACE: Auburn Hills, MI

DESIGNER: Chrysler Group, LLC

SPECIALTY: This lightening-fast drift car—with a huge rear wing, special body work, and race car interior—is made for burnin' out sideways!

'70 FORD ESCORT RS1600

BIRTHPLACE: Dearborn, MI
DESIGNER: Ford Motor Company
SPECIALTY: This sporty, compact Ford Escort can take whatever comes its way!

'13 CHEVROLET COPO CAMARO®

BIRTHPLACE: Detroit, MI
DESIGNER: General Motors
SPECIALTY: Featuring a roll cage, straight axle conversion, drag slips, and unique striping, with a 525-horse, 350 LSX engine and a 2.9L supercharger, this model is quite possibly more powerful than is stylishly possible.

FAST FACT

The Central Office Production Order or COPO Camaro was designed for drag racing action. Only 69 of them were produced!

SKY KNIFE®

BIRTHPLACE: El Segundo, CA

DESIGNER: Hot Wheels®

SPECIALTY: Tear up the skies with this jet-powered helicopter, featuring both a rooftop propeller and double jets.

HW RAPID RESPONDER™

BIRTHPLACE: El Segundo, CA

DESIGNER: Hot Wheels®

SPECIALTY: This updated Hot Wheels® classic is sure to be first on the scene!

RAPID RESPONSE

BIRTHPLACE: El Segundo, CA
DESIGNER: Hot Wheels®
SPECIALTY: Speed onto the scene and save the day with this souped-up rescue rod—complete with crash-rail fenders, light bar, and Hot Wheels® upgrades.

STREET STEALTH®

BIRTHPLACE: El Segundo, CA
DESIGNER: Hot Wheels®
SPECIALTY: This speed cycle is fast, sleek, and agile. With aerodynamic front fairings and a lightweight frame, it's street ready and always eager to accelerate.

BACKDRAFTER™

BIRTHPLACE: El Segundo, CA
DESIGNER: Hot Wheels®
SPECIALTY: A hot rod fire truck that really brings the heat. Twin engines, a rear spoiler, and all-terrain tires make sure this flame fighter can get anywhere fast.

BAD BAGGER™

BIRTHPLACE: El Segundo, CA
DESIGNER: Hot Wheels®
SPECIALTY: Load up the dual saddle bags and give the V-twin engine a rev—this motorcycle is ready to roll.

FLY-BY®

BIRTHPLACE: El Segundo, CA
DESIGNER: Hot Wheels®
SPECIALTY: Check out this fighter-jet bike with V-shaped rear wings and a turbine engine for record-busting speed—complete with an airbrake behind the seat!

TREASURE HUNT AND
SUPER TREASURE HUNT CARS

Hard to Find and Highly Collectible!

Take your Hot Wheels® collection to the next level with these tricked-out and rare paint schemes. Whether it's a limited-edition Corvette™ covered in flames or a souped-up version of a Hot Wheels® classic like Bone Shaker®, Treasure Hunt cars are the exclusive cars other collectors will envy. Check out these elusive racers and see what makes them so special, but keep an eye out for the even harder to find Super Treasure Hunt cars. Do you have any of these treasures in your collection?

MAD SPLASH®
2015 TREASURE HUNT

'69 CORVETTE®

T.H. YEAR: 2012
BIRTHPLACE: Detroit, MI
DESIGNER: General Motors
SPECIALTY: This updated paint scheme of a classic Corvette® sets this exclusive version apart from the pack!

CHECK OUT THE 2014 TREASURE HUNT ON PAGE 72.

SURF CRATE®

T.H. YEAR: 2012
BIRTHPLACE: El Segundo, CA
DESIGNER: Hot Wheels®
SPECIALTY: A hot rod primed for high speed, this woody catches the perfect wave with dual side exhausts, body-colored scoop, and removable surfboards!

'70 CHEVELLE™ SS™ WAGON

S.T.H. YEAR: 2012
BIRTHPLACE: Detroit, MI
DESIGNER: General Motors
SPECIALTY: Made for maximum versatility, this muscle car packs extra punch with a huge horsepower range.

PROTOTYPE H-24®

T.H. YEAR: 2013
BIRTHPLACE: El Segundo, CA
DESIGNER: Hot Wheels®
SPECIALTY: With lightweight construction and a 16-cylinder engine, this endurance car was made for long-distance racing with a team of drivers.

'69 CAMARO®

S.T.H. YEAR: 2013
BIRTHPLACE: Detroit, MI
DESIGNER: General Motors
SPECIALTY: With covered headlights and a cowl induction hood, this classic was made for racing to the beach.

'64 LINCOLN CONTINENTAL

T.H. YEAR: 2013
BIRTHPLACE: Dearborn, MI
DESIGNER: Ford Motor Company
SPECIALTY: Ride slow and low in this cruiser! Its squared off roofline, long body, and a V8 engine are sure to turn some heads.

CARBONATOR®

T.H. YEAR: 2013
BIRTHPLACE: El Segundo, CA
DESIGNER: Hot Wheels®
SPECIALTY: Designed to look like a soda bottle, Carbonator® is a hot rod with a huge rear wing and a turbine engine. This hot rod is sure to "pop" your top!

STING ROD II®

T.H. YEAR: 2013
BIRTHPLACE: El Segundo, CA
DESIGNER: Hot Wheels®
SPECIALTY: Don't mess with this fighter! This beast is always battle ready, with a saw blade in the rear, armor plating, and missile launchers mounted on all sides!

'09 CORVETTE® ZR1™

S.T.H. YEAR: 2013
BIRTHPLACE: Detroit, MI
DESIGNER: General Motors
SPECIALTY: Complete with rocker extensions, front air splitter, and a clear-domed hood to view the supercharged V8 engine, this Corvette® is clearly king of the road.

'73 FORD FALCON XB

S.T.H. YEAR: 2013
BIRTHPLACE: Dearborn, MI
DESIGNER: Ford Motor Company
SPECIALTY: With fat muscular lines, Ford V8 engine and front spoiler, and hood scoops, this Australian muscle car was made for Down Under duels.

CIRCLE TRUCKER®

T.H. YEAR: 2013
BIRTHPLACE: El Segundo, CA
DESIGNER: Hot Wheels®
SPECIALTY: This streamlined truck version of a modern favorite features an oversized cowl induction hood for max power, and a large wing keeps it planted on the track.

FIRE-EATER®

T.H. YEAR: 2013
BIRTHPLACE: El Segundo, CA
DESIGNER: Hot Wheels®
SPECIALTY: This customized fire engine heats up the streets while saving the day. It's fully stocked with water pumps, fire hoses, and ladders.

'71 DODGE DEMON

S.T.H. YEAR: 2013
BIRTHPLACE: Auburn Hills, MI
DESIGNER: Chrysler Group, LLC
SPECIALTY: With dual hood scoops, dual exhaust, and a 4-barrel carburetor, this powerful speed demon will possess the competition!

'07 FORD MUSTANG

S.T.H. YEAR: 2013
BIRTHPLACE: Dearborn, MI
DESIGNER: Ford Motor Company
SPECIALTY: Featuring special front and rear bumpers, a rear air diffuser, and a ducktail-style spoiler, this customized version of the standard '07 Mustang GT is ready to roll.

CHECK OUT ANOTHER VERSION ON PAGE 70.

BREAD BOX®

T.H. YEAR: 2013
BIRTHPLACE: El Segundo, CA
DESIGNER: Hot Wheels®
SPECIALTY: Powered by a lightweight, fuel-efficient turbocharged 4-banger, this speedy truck "delivers" every time!

BONE SHAKER®

S.T.H. YEAR: 2013
BIRTHPLACE: El Segundo, CA
DESIGNER: Hot Wheels®
SPECIALTY: The off-road version of a Hot Wheels® classic, complete with skull grille and skeleton-hand headlight casings. It's sure to scare up the dust!

'12 FORD FIESTA

T.H. YEAR: 2013
BIRTHPLACE: Dearborn, MI,
DESIGNER: Ford Motor Company
SPECIALTY: It has the front spoiler, chunky side skirts, and a turbocharged four-cylinder engine that makes this a souped-up Fiesta—but its flashy red paint scheme make it a treasure!

TAKE A LOOK AT THE FIESTA'S SNOW GEAR ON PAGE 46.

BAD TO THE BLADE®

T.H. YEAR: 2013
BIRTHPLACE: El Segundo, CA
DESIGNER: Hot Wheels®
SPECIALTY: Cut through the competition with this futuristic open-wheel racer. Designed for high speed with a supertorque engine and fins for downforce, it's one to watch.

'67 CAMARO®

S.T.H. YEAR: 2013
BIRTHPLACE: Detroit, MI
DESIGNER: General Motors
SPECIALTY: Its open hood, zoomy pipes, and a small-block V8 engine make this classic pony a "must-have" for the Hot Wheels® Dream Garage®.

'72 FORD GRAN TORINO SPORT

TH

S.T.H. YEAR: 2013
BIRTHPLACE: Dearborn, MI
DESIGNER: Ford Motor Company
SPECIALTY: With a V8 engine, dual exhaust, and a hood scoop, this muscle car was made for the "grand" stand.

'10 CAMARO® SS™

T.H. YEAR: 2013
BIRTHPLACE: Detroit, MI
DESIGNER: General Motors
SPECIALTY: With independent rear suspension for improved handling and a V8 engine, now everyone can own an actual General Motors concept car.

'62 CORVETTE®

TH

S.T.H. YEAR: 2013
BIRTHPLACE: Detroit, MI
DESIGNER: Ford Motor Company
SPECIALTY: A low-riding, two-seater classic, this racer sports not only the TH label under the side stripes but the Corvette logo on the hood!

'72 FORD RANCHERO

S.T.H. YEAR: 2013

BIRTHPLACE: Dearborn, MI

DESIGNER: Ford Motor Company

SPECIALTY: This retro two-door coupe utility truck puts a new twist on the station wagon by integrating the cab and cargo bed into the body.

FAST FACT

In 1972, there was a radical change in the Ranchero's design! The previously sleek, pointy look was replaced with a bolder design and the famous fishmouth grille.

FORD MUSTANG GT CONCEPT

T.H. YEAR: 2013

BIRTHPLACE: Dearborn, MI

DESIGNER: Ford Motor Company

SPECIALTY: Supercharged with a V8 engine, this full equipped pony is ready for a chase.

'71 EL CAMINO

T.H. YEAR: 2013
BIRTHPLACE: Detroit, MI
DESIGNER: General Motors
SPECIALTY: An essential part of any Hot Wheels®
garage, the '71 El Camino, with its cowl induction
hood and open back, is ready to roll!

FAST FACT

The El Camino was designed
as a sedan-pickup. In
North America, it is
classified as a
truck.

SPEEDBOX®

T.H. YEAR: 2014
BIRTHPLACE: El Segundo, CA
DESIGNER: Hot Wheels®
SPECIALTY: With a wide body for ground-hugging handling,
twin turbos, and all-wheel
drive, this extra-large
bruiser is fully
loaded and
brings the
heat.

'64 CHEVY® NOVA™ STATION WAGON

S.T.H. YEAR: 2014
BIRTHPLACE: Detroit, MI
DESIGNER: General Motors
SPECIALTY: This old-school delivery wagon was offered in V4, V6, or V8 versions, so you could "order your economy as lively as you wanted it."

CLOAK AND DAGGER®

T.H. YEAR: 2014
BIRTHPLACE: El Segundo, CA
DESIGNER: Hot Wheels®
SPECIALTY: Lean, mean, and green! This single-seater got an out-of-this-world paint scheme for its Treasure Hunt run.

RACE TO PAGE 23 TO SEE AN ALL NEW PAINT SCHEME!

LOOP COUPE®

T.H. YEAR: 2014
BIRTHPLACE: El Segundo, CA
DESIGNER: Hot Wheels®
SPECIALTY: It's no surprise that this insanely fast racer was inspired by Super Blitzen®, a 2010 Hot Wheels® original—both Loop Coupe® and Super Blitzen® were built for speed!

CHEVY® SILVERADO™

S.T.H. YEAR: 2014
BIRTHPLACE: Detroit, MI
DESIGNER: General Motors
SPECIALTY: Whether you're hauling a sport bike for an impromptu two-wheel race or burning up the streets in a road race, this slammed truck is up to the challenge.

S.T.H. YEAR: 2014
BIRTHPLACE: Detroit, MI
DESIGNER: General Motors
SPECIALTY: Check out this full-scale Hot Wheels® Camaro, with real-life red line tires, super shiny paint, and Hot Wheels® badging—available in V6 or V8, coupe or convertible. Ready to play?

FAST FACT

Hot Wheels® and Camaro® have teamed up since the beginning! One of the first 16 Hot Wheels®, created in 1968, was a Custom Camaro®.

'76 GREENWOOD CORVETTE® *TH*

S.T.H. YEAR: 2014
BIRTHPLACE: Detroit, MI
DESIGNER: General Motors
SPECIALTY: Its unique covered head lights, rear spoiler, and side exhaust make this Corvette® stand out from the pack.

'07 FORD MUSTANG

S.T.H. YEAR: 2014
BIRTHPLACE: Dearborn, MI
DESIGNER: Ford Motor Company
SPECIALTY: Featuring special front and rear bumpers, a rear air diffuser, and a ducktail-style spoiler, this customized version of the standard '07 Mustang GT is ready to roll.

CHECK OUT ANOTHER SUPER TREASURE HUNT VERSION ON PAGE 61.

'65 CHEVY® IMPALA™

S.T.H. YEAR: 2014
BIRTHPLACE: Detroit, MI
DESIGNER: General Motors
SPECIALTY: Slammed low and ready to go, this cruiser has classic Impala™ styling with round triple taillights, curved side glass, and rear quarter emblems.

FANGSTER®

T.H. YEAR: 2014
BIRTHPLACE: El Segundo, CA
DESIGNER: Hot Wheels®
SPECIALTY: Unleash this monster racer! Its distinctive design is a collector's dream . . .
or nightmare!

NIGHT BURNER®

T.H. YEAR: 2014
BIRTHPLACE: El Segundo, CA
DESIGNER: Hot Wheels®
SPECIALTY: Take it out for a spin and listen to it scream. Thanks to an impressive turbine engine, this car literally leaves the competition's ears burning!

'69 CORVETTE®

S.T.H. YEAR: 2014

BIRTHPLACE: Detroit, MI

DESIGNER: General Motors

SPECIALTY: Based on the actual production model, with classic Corvette® styling, a lighter body, and a beefy all-aluminum engine block, the elusive ZL-1 has raced its way to the head of the pack!

RACE OVER TO PAGE 54 TO SEE ANOTHER STYLIN' LOOK.

OFF TRACK®

T.H. YEAR: 2014

BIRTHPLACE: El Segundo, CA

DESIGNER: Hot Wheels®

SPECIALTY: With its custom chrome-moly frame and low center of gravity, this all-terrain pickup can handle any obstacle. It's a dirt-racing pro that knows how to get places quickly!

MUSTANG MACH 1

S.T.H. YEAR: 2014

BIRTHPLACE: Dearborn, MI

DESIGNER: Ford Motor Company

SPECIALTY: With a hood-mounted tachometer, hood scoop, and a Cobra jet engine, this muscle car was made to pull some serious Gs!

CUSTOM '71 EL CAMINO™

T.H. YEAR: 2014

BIRTHPLACE: Detroit, MI

DESIGNER: General Motors, with help from Hot Wheels® Test Facility

SPECIALTY: This custom classic vehicle is an unstoppable force, with twin jet engines and custom wheels that can withstand speeds above 400 mph (643 km/h). It's ready to take off. Are you?

CHEVROLET SS *TH*

S.T.H. YEAR: 2014
BIRTHPLACE: Detroit, MI
DESIGNER: General Motors
SPECIALTY: With its racing stripes, dual exhaust, hood bulges to show off its power and a V8 engine, this American classic is one mean muscle car!

LA FASTA®

T.H. YEAR: 2014
BIRTHPLACE: El Segundo, CA
DESIGNER: Hot Wheels®
SPECIALTY: With a roof-mounted intake, transparent engine cover, and supercharged V8 engine, this European exotic is one fast puppy!

RESCUE DUTY®

T.H. YEAR: 2014
BIRTHPLACE: El Segundo, CA
DESIGNER: Hot Wheels®
SPECIALTY: Built for speed, this hardworking rescue vehicle is there when it's most important.

'55 CHEVY® BEL AIR GASSER

S.T.H. YEAR: 2014
BIRTHPLACE: Detroit, MI
DESIGNER: General Motors
SPECIALTY: It's a true blast from the past! This classic gasser is powered by a blown big-block engine, while its open fender headers and stripped interior give it extra style.

STOCKAR

T.H. YEAR: 2014
BIRTHPLACE: El Segundo, CA
DESIGNER: Hot Wheels®
SPECIALTY: This stock car tears up the oval track with its cowl induction hood, V8 engine, and streamlined shape for perfect aerodynamics.

CHECK OUT ANOTHER STYLIN' LOOK ON PAGE 21.

75

POISON ARROW®

T.H. YEAR: 2014
BIRTHPLACE: El Segundo, CA
DESIGNER: Hot Wheels®
SPECIALTY: Super-stealthy and streamlined, this vehicle is perfect for top-secret missions. Its rear propeller, dual rudders, and high-visibility cockpit are ready for takeoff.

TWIN MILL®

S.T.H. YEAR: 2014
BIRTHPLACE: El Segundo, CA
DESIGNER: Hot Wheels®
SPECIALTY: Dual big blocks and front intakes give this supercharged racer twice as much speed!

FAST FACT

Twin Mill® is one of the most popular castings—so popular there are two variations called Twin Mill® II and Twin Mill® III!

SANDBLASTER®

S.T.H. YEAR: 2014

BIRTHPLACE: Dearborn, MI

DESIGNER: Ford Motor Company

SPECIALTY: This desert-ready off-roader, with its V8 engine, prerunner style suspension, roll cage, custom hood and fenders, and skid plates, will leave a sandstorm in its wake!

MAXIMUM LEEWAY®

T.H. YEAR: 2014

BIRTHPLACE: El Segundo, CA

DESIGNER: Hot Wheels®

SPECIALTY: This powerful, streamlined racer, with 850 hp and a V8 engine, can drift sideways at over 100 mph (160 km/h). Watch out! This bad boy needs some room to maneuver!

'70 CHEVY® CHEVELLE™ SS

TH

S.T.H. YEAR: 2014
BIRTHPLACE: Detroit, MI
DESIGNER: General Motors
SPECIALTY: A muscle car with extra punch, the Chevelle™ was made for maximum versatility and huge horsepower range.

TWINDUCTION®

T.H. YEAR: 2014
BIRTHPLACE: El Segundo, CA
DESIGNER: Hot Wheels®
SPECIALTY: This revved-up version of a Hot Wheels® classic muscle car has a large rear spoiler, wide wheel fenders, twin induction manifold, and a 485-hp engine!

FAST FACT

Twinduction® is part of the Hot Wheels® Glow Wheels line, with glow-in-the-dark wheels that make it easy to spot.

ENFORCER®

T.H. YEAR: 2015
BIRTHPLACE: El Segundo, CA
DESIGNER: Hot Wheels®
SPECIALTY: Off-road recon is no problem for this single-seater buggy. It can face any challenge with its side-mounted machine guns and roof-mounted missles.

8 CRATE®

S.T.H. YEAR: 2015
BIRTHPLACE: El Segundo, CA
DESIGNER: Hot Wheels®
SPECIALTY: With a powerful V8 engine under the hood and rear fin fenders, this wagon is a classic cruiser.

'70 PLYMOUTH SUPERBIRD

S.T.H. YEAR: 2015
BIRTHPLACE: Detroit, MI
DESIGNER: Chrysler Group, LLC
SPECIALTY: With custom nose and rear wing and V8 426 HEMI®
engine, this modified Road Runner® was made to fly the coop.

ROGUE HOG™

T.H. YEAR: 2015
BIRTHPLACE: El Segundo, CA
DESIGNER: Hot Wheels®
SPECIALTY: Built with high-speed and high-tech specs,
you'll think you're traveling through time in this futuristic
fun machine.

FAST FELION®

T.H. YEAR: 2015
BIRTHPLACE: El Segundo, CA
DESIGNER: Hot Wheels®
SPECIALTY: This European-style 2-seat GT coupe, with a twin turbo V8 engine, tears up the streets with its speed. *Meow.* This is one cool cat!

FAST FACT
Fast FeLion® was the inspiration behind the 2014 Rrroadster.

TIME TRACKER®

T.H. YEAR: 2015
BIRTHPLACE: El Segundo, CA
DESIGNER: Hot Wheels®
SPECIALTY: This highly modified, aerodynamic 900-hp racer dominates the street and the clock!

MAD SPLASH®

T.H. YEAR: 2015
BIRTHPLACE: El Segundo,CA
DESIGNER: Hot Wheels®
SPECIALTY: This amphibious vehicle owes its heritage to the classic Hot Wheels® favorite, Madfast®. It's fast and agile—on land or water.

FAST FACT

The airless tires on Rocketfire® roll on a unique webbed design that gets rid of the need to pump air into your wheels—making flat tires a thing of the past.

ROCKETFIRE™

T.H. YEAR: 2015
BIRTHPLACE: El Segundo, CA
DESIGNER: Hot Wheels®
SPECIALTY: Blast off with an out-of-this-world, rocket-powered racer! With aileron guides, airless tires, and gravity-fed fuel pods, it's ready for an interstellar adventure.

JET THREAT™ 4

T.H. YEAR: 2015
BIRTHPLACE: El Segundo, CA
DESIGNER: Hot Wheels®
SPECIALTY: This extreme flier
has a vertical stabilizer,
fold-down wings, and
dual jet engines that can
transform it from a ground
racer to an airborne threat.

CUSTOM '77 DODGE VAN *TH*

S.T.H. YEAR: 2015
BIRTHPLACE: Auburn Hills, MI
DESIGNER: Chrysler Group, LLC
SPECIALTY: Turn up the beats and
rock out with this "super"
custom paint scheme.

RRROADSTER *TH*

S.T.H. YEAR: 2015
BIRTHPLACE: El Segundo, CA
DESIGNER: Hot Wheels®
SPECIALTY: The 5.0L V8,
supercharged 600-hp engine
and open cockpit in this
British-style roadster are sure
to blow your hair back!

FAST GASSIN®

T.H. YEAR: 2015
BIRTHPLACE: El Segundo, CA
DESIGNER: Hot Wheels®
SPECIALTY: This hot-rodded fuel tanker with 8 vertical stacks, 6 wheels, and 3 axles makes sure you're never on empty!

'69 FORD MUSTANG BOSS 302

S.T.H. YEAR: 2015
BIRTHPLACE: Dearborn, MI
DESIGNER: Ford Motor Company
SPECIALTY: Originally produced in1969 and 1970, the boss is back in the base form of a 2011 Mustang GT. Think it was worth the wait? Some say it's the best Mustang ever!

PARADIGM SHIFT®

T.H. YEAR: 2015
BIRTHPLACE: El Segundo, CA
DESIGNER: Hot Wheels®
SPECIALTY: Shift into high gear with this turbocharged 4-cylinder tuner car! Its big wing and side air intakes give it extra style.

PASS'N GASSER®

S.T.H. YEAR: 2015
BIRTHPLACE: Dearborn, MI
DESIGNER: Ford Motor Company
SPECIALTY: With race-injector stacks and a parachute, this single-seat drag racer will make the competition "pass out" from defeat!

REDONDO BEACH, CA

Reyna & Cook

CHICANE®

T.H. YEAR: 2015
BIRTHPLACE: El Segundo, CA
DESIGNER: Hot Wheels®
SPECIALTY: With 400 hp and a turbocharged 3.5-litre mid-mounted V6, this mean machine will stop at nothing to beat the competition.

FAST FACT

A chicane is an artificial notch in a straightaway, creating extra turns in a road.

PIRANHA TERROR®

T.H. YEAR: 2015
BIRTHPLACE: El Segundo, CA
DESIGNER: Hot Wheels®
SPECIALTY: With big tires and a heavy build, this solid little car is ready to chomp down the track. Add in fins for ultimate maneuvering, it's a total terror.

TREAD AIR®

T.H. YEAR: 2015
BIRTHPLACE: El Segundo, CA
DESIGNER: Hot Wheels®
SPECIALTY: Twin-turbine engines give this jet-inspired, high-speed off-roader its power. Rolling on a mono-tread, this high flyer is ready to take on uncharted territory!

'65 MUSTANG 2+2 FASTBACK

S.T.H. YEAR: 2015
BIRTHPLACE: Dearborn, MI
DESIGNER: Ford Motor Company
SPECIALTY: Redefine the term "sports car" with this Ford classic. It revolutionized the automotive industry with its sporty styling, V8 engine, and custom exhaust.

TEAM HOT WHEELS® CORKSCREW BUGGY

T.H. YEAR: 2015
BIRTHPLACE: El Segundo, CA
DESIGNER: Team Hot Wheels®
SPECIALTY: This high-performance buggy completed its record-breaking corkscrew jump in 2012. Reaching 54 mph (87 km/h) before hitting the jump, it rotated 230 degrees per second and then touched down 92 feet (28 m) later!

'10 PRO STOCK CAMARO®

S.T.H. YEAR: 2016
BIRTHPLACE: Detroit, MI
DESIGNER: General Motors
SPECIALTY: As a member of the HW Mild to Wild™ mini collection, this souped-up custom Camaro® is ready to push the limits of speed!

'14 CORVETTE® STINGRAY™

TH

S.T.H. YEAR: 2016
BIRTHPLACE: Detroit, MI
DESIGNER: General Motors
SPECIALTY: With nearly 450 hp, this styling racer is sure to leave its competition with a sting!

RACE TO PAGE 32 TO SEE THE TREASURE HUNT VERSION.

4WARD SPEED®

T.H. YEAR: 2016
BIRTHPLACE: El Segundo, CA
DESIGNER: Hot Wheels®
SPECIALTY: This futuristic racer, featuring a narrow cockpit, twin turbo engines, and a back wing, is built for speed and ready for takeoff!

RIP ROD®

T.H. YEAR: 2016
BIRTHPLACE: El Segundo, CA
DESIGNER: Hot Wheels®
SPECIALTY: Reaching top speeds of 125 mph (201 km/h), this ripper is not only a 2016 Treasure Hunt car but a member of the HW Glow Wheels™ mini collection. Watch out for its fang-like exhaust tips and mask-like grille.

FAST FACT

While behind the wheel of Rip Rod®, Red Driver was crowned champion in Hot Wheels® World's Best Driver.

'11 CORVETTE GRAND SPORT

T.H. YEAR: 2016
BIRTHPLACE: Detroit, MI
DESIGNER: General Motors
SPECIALTY: Wide-body styling meets racing-bred suspension in this baby. Plus improved fuel economy means it can spend weekends at the track and still do 9-to-5 in style.

MIG RIG®

T.H. YEAR: 2016
BIRTHPLACE: El Segundo, CA
DESIGNER: Hot Wheels®
SPECIALTY: Who says you can't work hard and get there in quick style? This retro-style pickup designed by Larry Wood has a mid-mounted V8 motor and plenty of welding tools in the back.

MOUNTAIN MAULER®

T.H. YEAR: 2016
BIRTHPLACE: El Segundo, CA
DESIGNER: Hot Wheels®
SPECIALTY: A formula off-road racer designed with one thing in mind—getting up the mountainside as fast a sit can. Let it rip and watch it get dirty!

BOOM BOX®

S.T.H. YEAR: 2016
BIRTHPLACE: El Segundo, CA
DESIGNER: Hot Wheels®
SPECIALTY: Make a splash in this low-riding, mini collection HW Art Car™. Crank up the beats on its rockin' sound system and take it for a spin.

GLOSSARY

AERODYNAMIC: Shaped in a way that reduces drag.

AWD/4WD: An AWD (all-wheel-drive) or 4WD (four-wheel-drive) vehicle is a four-wheeled vehicle with a drivetrain that allows all four wheels to receive torque from the engine.

BLOWN ENGINE: An engine that is equipped with a supercharger, also known as a blower.

CHASSIS: The base frame of a car or other wheeled vehicle.

CHICANE: An artificial feature creating extra turns in a road, used in motor racing and on streets to slow traffic for safety.

COWL INDUCTION: An opening in the hood that forces air into the engine for cooling.

DOWNFORCE: A result of gravity and air flowing over a moving vehicle that pushes it into the ground and stabilizes it.

DRAG: (1) A slowing force caused by air flowing over a shape. **(2)** A short distance—as in race down the drag.

DRAGSTER (DRAG CAR): An automobile designed and built specifically for drag racing.

DRIFTER (DRIFT CAR): A car designed to slide when the driver uses throttle, brakes, clutch, gear shifting, and steering to keep the car in a high-turn angle.

GRAND TOURER (GT): A luxury car designed for high speeds and long distances.

GRILLE: The grating at the front of the car that allows air to circulate to the radiator for cooling.

HOT ROD: Slang term for a car specially built or altered for fast acceleration and increased speed.

LOW-DRAG BODY: The design of a car that produces less drag so it can go faster.

MUSCLE CAR: A flashy sports car with a large, powerful engine.

OFF-ROAD: A vehicle designed for use over rough terrain.

SIDE EXHAUST: An exhaust pipe designed to carry toxic gases away from the car, specifically out the side rather than the back.

SOLAR POWERED: Powered solely by the sun's rays.

SOUPED UP: Any vehicle that has been modified or upgraded for performance or looks.

SPOILER: An air deflector usually mounted at the rear of a car to reduce lift at high speeds.

TORQUE: A force that produces rotation.

TUNER CAR: A vehicle that is reworked and built on to in order to create maximum power.

TWIN TURBO: An engine with two turbochargers, common in muscle cars and racers.

WIND SPLITTER: A protruding flat surface at the front of a car, designed to decrease front-end lift and exert downforce.

WINGS: Structures added to generate downforce or downward motion, making the car more stable as it accelerates or gains speed.

Trivia

(Answers are on the bottom of page 95)

1 FROM WHICH CAR IS THIS DETAIL?

2 WHAT DOES THIS MINI COLLECTIONS SYMBOL STAND FOR?

3 IN WHICH HOT WHEELS® MINI COLLECTION ARE BAD MUDDER™ II, OFF DUTY®, AND DAWGZILLA™?

4 SPOILERS PERFORM WHAT FUNCTION ON A CAR?

A. Vent fumes
B. Let air enter the car and protect the engine
C. Allow better airflow over and around the car
D. Help absorb shock

5 WHICH CAR WAS MADE FOR INTERPLANETARY STEALTH MISSIONS?

A. Cloak and Dagger®
B. Power Surge™
C. Paradigm Shift®
D. Tread Air®